PERSPECTIVES ON
AMERICAN PROGRESS

THE LEGALIZATION OF SAME-SEX MARRIAGE

BY DUCHESS HARRIS, JD, PHD

WITH CHRISTINA ESCHBACH

Cover image: Jim Obergefell and supporters celebrated the Supreme Court decision in 2015 to allow same-sex marriage nationwide.

Core Library

An Imprint of Abdo Publishing
abdopublishing.com

abdopublishing.com

Published by Abdo Publishing, a division of ABDO, PO Box 398166, Minneapolis, Minnesota 55439. Copyright © 2019 by Abdo Consulting Group, Inc. International copyrights reserved in all countries. No part of this book may be reproduced in any form without written permission from the publisher. Core Library™ is a trademark and logo of Abdo Publishing.

Printed in the United States of America, North Mankato, Minnesota
032018
092018

Cover Photo: Eric Gay/AP Images
Interior Photos: Eric Gay/AP Images, 1; Jacquelyn Martin/AP Images, 4–5; Rena Schild/ Shutterstock Images, 7; Red Line Editorial, 11, 24; Dennis Cook/AP Images, 12; Donna Aceto/ Polaris/Newscom, 14–15; Joe Tabacca/Sipa USA/Newscom, 18, 43; Pete Marovich/UPI/ Newscom, 20–21; Kevin Lamarque/Reuters/Newscom, 22; ZUMA Press, Inc./Alamy, 26–27; Damian Dovarganes/AP Images, 28; Dana Verkouteren/AP Images, 30; Jacquelyn Martin/AP Images, 34–35; Kim Kulish/Corbis Historical/Getty Images, 37; David Gray/Reuters/Newscom, 39; Erik McGregor/ Pacific Press/Newscom, 40

Editor: Claire Vanden Branden
Imprint Designer: Maggie Villaume
Series Design Direction: Ryan Gale

Library of Congress Control Number: 2017962653

Publisher's Cataloging-in-Publication Data

Names: Harris, Duchess, author. | Eschbach, Christina, author.
Title: The legalization of same-sex marriage / by Duchess Harris and Christina Eschbach.
Description: Minneapolis, Minnesota : Abdo Publishing, 2019. | Series: Perspectives on American progress | Includes online resources and index.
Identifiers: ISBN 9781532114939 (lib.bdg.) | ISBN 9781532154768 (ebook)
Subjects: LCSH: Same-sex marriage--Law and legislation--United States—Juvenile literature. | Conflict of laws--Same-sex marriage--Juvenile literature. | Same-sex marriage-Juvenile literature.
Classification: DDC 346.730168--dc23

CONTENTS

CHAPTER
ONE

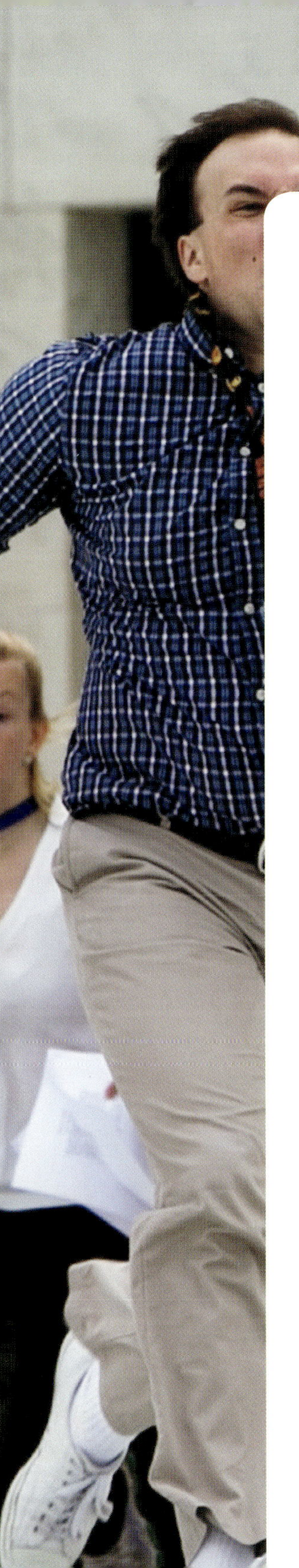

MAKING SAME-SEX MARRIAGE LEGAL

t was a blazing hot morning on June 26, 2015, in Washington, DC. Still, a crowd of people stood in the heat outside the Supreme Court building. They were waiting to hear about an important decision. It would change the lives of millions of Americans. The news would come through a Washington tradition known as the Running of the Interns.

The Supreme Court does not allow recording devices. This means the fastest way

Interns have to run approximately 300 feet (90 m) from the Supreme Court building to the press outside.

to get news out is with paper copies. In the Running of the Interns, members of the media dash from the court to their news teams. Then the news of the court's outcome is broken to the public.

On this morning, the court had made a decision in the case of *Obergefell v. Hodges*. This could legalize same-sex marriage across the country. An intern for the news channel CNBC delivered the news first. In a 5 to 4 decision, the Supreme Court had given same-sex couples the right to marry.

The History of LGBT Rights

In the 1960s, many people viewed homosexuality as a mental illness. Most Christians viewed it as immoral. Relationships between men were illegal in many states. People who were gay often lost their jobs. They were treated poorly by their families and friends.

People in the gay community often gathered at bars. There, they could be themselves without fear. However, police often arrested many people at

The White House lit up with rainbow colors, the gay pride emblem, the night of the *Obergefell* ruling.

these bars. One bar was the Stonewall Inn in Greenwich Village, New York. What happened there on June 28, 1969, started the gay rights movement.

Usually people left bars after arrests were made. However, this night was different. People outside the bar became angry. They started throwing garbage at the police.

In response, the police officers locked themselves inside the bar. They called for help. As the night went on, someone set fire to the Stonewall Inn. The fire department arrived and put the fire out. Then they rescued the police. Nearly 400 people joined in the fighting.

The Stonewall riots were a key moment in LGBT history. A year later, people in major cities held parades to remember the event. These events brought the gay community together. Many groups were formed to help gay people gain rights.

Over the next few decades, legal cases shaped the progress of gay rights. Many states had laws against male same-sex relationships. Women were rarely included in these laws. These laws had been in place since colonial times. They carried punishment of prison or death. In 1986, the Supreme Court ruled that relationships between men were not protected by

FIRST AMERICAN GAY RIGHTS ORGANIZATION

The first gay rights organization was the Society for Human Rights. It was founded in 1924 in Chicago, Illinois. A German immigrant, Henry Gerber, started the group. He wanted to protect the rights of gay people. However, it attracted very few members. Being gay was not widely accepted in the United States. Gerber was arrested in 1925 for promoting his group. This marked the end of the Society for Human Rights.

the Constitution. This meant that states had the power to determine the law on this issue.

In 1990, three same-sex couples applied for marriage licenses in Hawaii. The applications were turned down. In response they filed a lawsuit. They argued that they were being discriminated against. The Hawaiian court dismissed the suit. The case was then brought to the Hawaii Supreme Court. The court agreed with the couples. This alarmed many people. At the time, 57 percent of people in the United States were against same-sex marriage. The Hawaiian Supreme Court later changed its opinion. Hawaii added a part to its constitution allowing only opposite-sex couples to marry.

People have been against same-sex marriage for different reasons. Some make religious arguments. Marriage ceremonies are often linked to religion. Many religions view homosexuality as immoral. Some people feel same-sex marriage is against their religion.

PUBLIC OPINION ON SAME-SEX MARRIAGE IN THE UNITED STATES

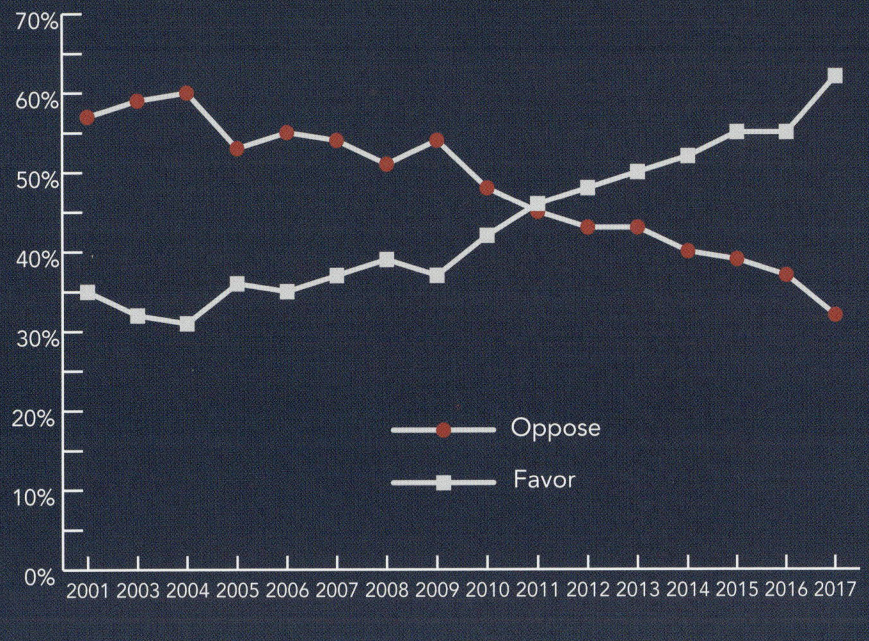

Others believe the goal of marriage is to have children. They oppose same-sex marriage for this reason. Some people argue that children need both a mother and a father.

People who were against same-sex marriage were in favor of the Defense of Marriage Act (DOMA). In 1996, Georgia representative Bob Barr introduced

Genora Dancel, *left*, and Ninia Baehr were two of the people who filed the lawsuit in Hawaii. Their decision paved the way for equal marriage rights later on.

this act. Senator Don Nickles of Oklahoma introduced a similar act in the Senate. This act said that no state had to recognize a same-sex marriage that was legal in another state. It also defined *marriage* as between a man and a woman. DOMA sparked a new generation to fight for marriage equality.

STRAIGHT TO THE
SOURCE

Justice Anthony Kennedy wrote the majority opinion for *Obergefell*. In it, he outlines the history of discrimination against gay and lesbian people in the United States:

> *Until the mid-20th century, same-sex intimacy long had been condemned as immoral. . . . For this reason, among others, many persons did not deem homosexuals to have dignity in their own distinct identity. A truthful declaration by same-sex couples of what was in their hearts had to remain unspoken. . . . Same-sex intimacy remained a crime in many states. Gays and lesbians were prohibited from most government employment, barred from military service, excluded under immigration laws, targeted by police, and burdened in their rights to associate.*

> Source: Justice Anthony Kennedy. "Read the Supreme Court Ruling That Recognized Gay Marriage Nationwide." *Time*. Time Inc., 26 June 2015. Web. December 20, 2017.

Back It Up
The author of this passage is using evidence to support a point. Write a paragraph describing the point the author is making. Then write down two or three pieces of evidence the author uses to make the point.

CHAPTER
TWO

TAKING ON DOMA

One major step in marriage equality came in 2013. In that year, the Supreme Court ruled on a case involving Edith Windsor. The case would pave the way for the later *Obergefell* ruling.

Windsor was a computer programmer. She met Thea Spyer in 1965. They soon began a relationship. Spyer proposed in 1967. But the idea of two women marrying was unthinkable for many people.

Before Stonewall, Windsor and Spyer had little interest in activism. Then the riots inspired them. Windsor later said that Stonewall "changed my life forever." Spyer and Windsor began new lives as activists. They marched in gay pride parades. These parades allowed LGBT people to openly express themselves. They joined gay rights groups. They worked for equality.

DOMA

In 1996, same-sex marriage rights suffered a setback. Congress passed DOMA. President Bill Clinton signed the law. DOMA said the federal government would not recognize same-sex marriages. Some states, however, still considered allowing same-sex marriages.

RIGHTS AND PRIVILEGES OF MARRIAGE

The right to marry is important because it provides many legal benefits. A spouse can make medical choices if the other cannot. Spouses can appear on birth and death certificates. Married couples pay less in taxes. Health insurance can be extended to a spouse. If a couple gets divorced, it is easier for a parent to get custody. If one person dies, the other can receive Social Security. It is easier for a citizen's foreign spouse to immigrate to the United States. Marriage also provides visiting rights in jail.

Marriage rights go beyond just a ceremony. They include important legal rights. For example, a married person can receive money from a partner without tax fines. Gay rights activists were strongly against DOMA. The law meant that couples like Windsor and Spyer could not have equal marriages.

Going to Court

Spyer died in 2009. Windsor inherited everything. New York recognized their marriage, but the US government did not. This meant Windsor had to pay hundreds of thousands of dollars in taxes. If she had married a man,

Windsor was named Grand Marshall in the 2013 New York City Gay Pride Parade.

she would not have paid anything. She filed a lawsuit to get these same rights.

The case eventually reached the Supreme Court. It was called *United States v. Windsor*. On June 26, 2013, the court ruled that Windsor would receive the money without being taxed. This struck down parts of DOMA.

It left other parts alone. The federal government no longer defined marriage as only between a man and a woman. However, individual states could still chose to not recognize same-sex marriages.

Windsor and other activists saw the importance of full marriage equality. At a 2009 rally in New York, she said, "*Married* is a magic word. And it is magic throughout the world. It has to do with our dignity as human beings, to be who we are openly."

FURTHER EVIDENCE

Chapter Two talks about Edith Windsor and the Defense of Marriage Act. What is one of the main points of this chapter? What evidence is included to support this point? Read the article at the website below. Does the information on this website support the chapter's main point?

FREQUENTLY ASKED QUESTIONS: DEFENSE OF MARRIAGE ACT (DOMA)
abdocorelibrary.com/same-sex-marriage

CHAPTER
THREE

JIM OBERGEFELL

Jim Obergefell was a computer consultant from Ohio. He met his partner, John Arthur, in the early 1990s. In February 2004, Ohio banned same-sex marriage. In 2011, Arthur was diagnosed with amyotrophic lateral sclerosis (ALS). After *United States v. Windsor* struck down part of DOMA, Obergefell and Arthur decided to get married. They married on July 11, 2013, in Maryland. There, same-sex marriage was legal. However, their marriage was not recognized by Ohio.

Jim Obergefell kept a photo of his deceased partner, John Arthur, in his pocket during the Supreme Court case.

Since the court ruling, Obergefell has spoken at many events, including the Democratic National Committee LGBT Gala in 2015 where he met President Barack Obama.

They both knew Arthur would die soon. This pushed Obergefell to file a lawsuit. He wanted his name on the death certificate. On July 22, 2013, a federal judge ruled in their favor. Obergefell's name would appear on the death certificate.

However, the battle was far from over. Arthur died on October 22, 2013. Obergefell's name appeared

on the certificate. But Ohio refused to recognize their
marriage. The state appealed to the United States Court
of Appeals for the Sixth District. That court reversed
the decision.

Obergefell then appealed to the Supreme Court. On January 16, 2015, the court accepted the case. It was combined with three similar cases. The court heard arguments from both sides on April 28, 2015.

The Court's Decision

Obergefell came to the court every day for a month. Finally, the decision was

FEDERAL COURT SYSTEM

There are three levels of the federal court system. District courts are the lowest level. Every state has at least one district court. District courts have juries that decide cases. People who lose cases in district courts can appeal to circuit courts. These are the next level. There are twelve circuit courts in the United States. In circuit courts, judges decide cases. Appealed cases from circuit courts go to the Supreme Court. Supreme Court justices decide these cases. Their decisions are final; they cannot be appealed.

SAME-SEX MARRIAGE BEFORE
OBERGEFELL

Many states had legalized same-sex marriage before *Obergefell*. In others, same-sex marriage was banned. The *Obergefell* decision made these bans illegal.

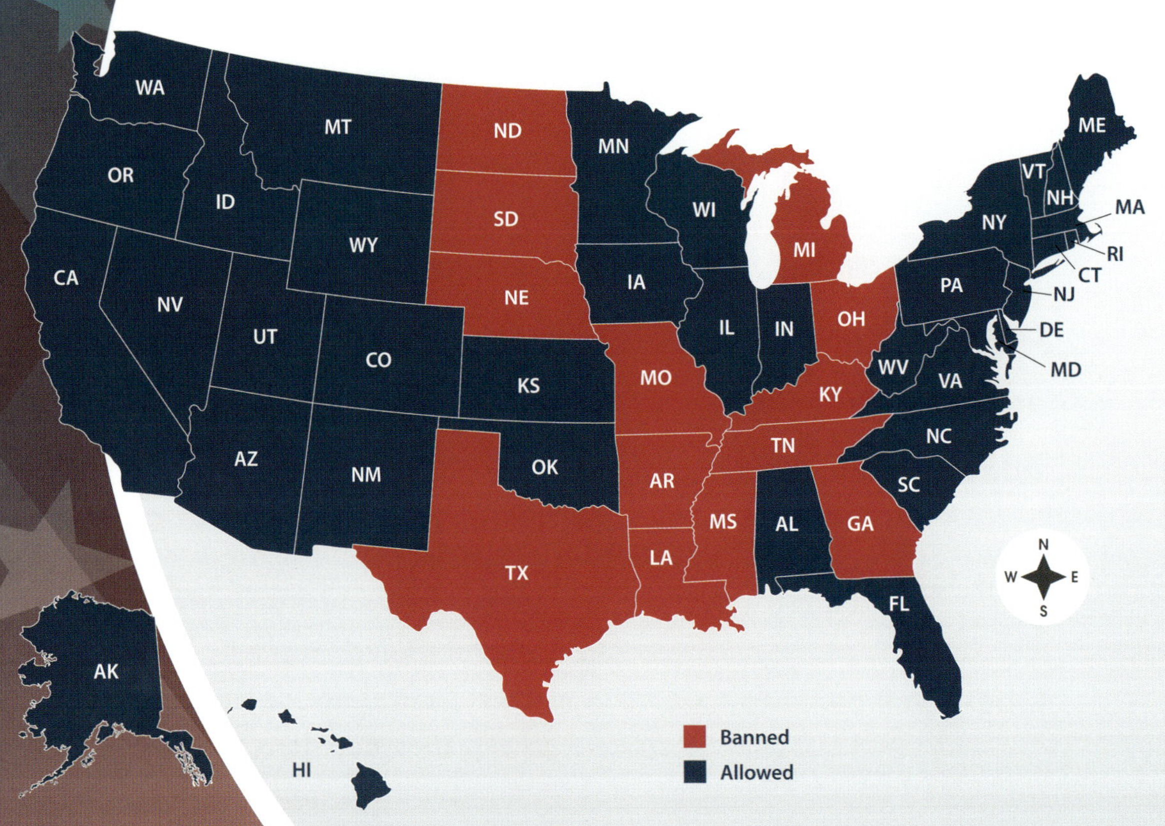

announced on June 26, 2015. The court ruled in his favor, 5 to 4. He was sitting in the courtroom while Justice Anthony Kennedy read the outcome. This struck down DOMA. Same-sex marriage was now legal in all states.

Outside the Supreme Court, Obergefell stood surrounded by supporters and cameras. Holding a picture of Arthur and smiling, he gave a speech on the importance of the decision. In his speech he said he now felt "like a real American."

CHAPTER
FOUR

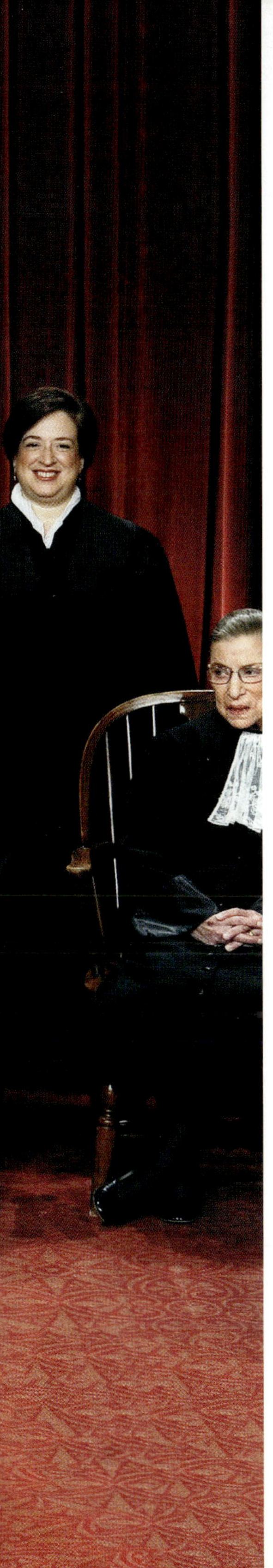

THE MAJORITY OPINION

The Supreme Court has nine judges. To decide a case, a majority of the judges must agree. When judges decide, they publish an opinion. This is a document that explains the reasoning behind their choice. To support their argument, they use previous cases and the Constitution.

The Fourteenth Amendment

Obergefell believed not issuing a marriage license to same-sex couples was against the Fourteenth Amendment. The Fourteenth Amendment says each state must give its people "equal protection of the laws."

Top row, left to right: Sonia Sotomayor, Stephen Breyer, Samuel Alito, Elena Kagan; front row: Clarence Thomas, Antonin Scalia, John Roberts, Anthony Kennedy, and Ruth Bader Ginsburg

He also argued that not recognizing his out-of-state marriage was against this amendment.

The five justices who agreed with Obergefell were Anthony Kennedy, Ruth Bader Ginsburg, Stephen Breyer, Elena Kagan, and Sonia Sotomayor. Justice Kennedy wrote the majority opinion.

SAME-SEX MARRIAGE IN MASSACHUSETTS

Gay and Lesbian Advocates and Defenders (GLAD) sued the Massachusetts Department of Public Health in April 2001. They filed a lawsuit on behalf of seven same-sex couples. These couples had been denied marriage licenses. A Massachusetts court ruled in the Department of Heath's favor. Then GLAD appealed to the Massachusetts Supreme Court. The court ruled that not issuing marriage licenses to same-sex couples violated the state constitution. This ruling made Massachusetts the first state to legalize same-sex marriage.

Anthony Kennedy has served as a Supreme Court justice since 1988.

Since photographers aren't allowed inside the Supreme Court, artists often draw illustrations of major cases.

Kennedy's Arguments

The justices looked at previous cases to support their choice. Kennedy mentioned four arguments. The first argument cited the case *Loving v. Virginia*. This 1967 case made laws against interracial marriage illegal. Justices in this case said people had the freedom to marry people of other races. Kennedy extended this idea to same-sex couples.

The second argument cited the 1965 case *Griswold v. Connecticut*. Connecticut banned the use of birth control. The court ruled that the law violated "the right of marital privacy." It said that marriage was a unique and special union. *Obergefell* said same-sex couples deserved these special rights, too.

The third argument made was that marriage protects children and families. Marriage provides strength and support to families. A good home life gives children a good environment to grow up in. When same-sex couples are not allowed to marry, their families may be seen as lesser than other families. Married couples receive tax benefits. This can mean same-sex couples may have less money than other couples. This can cause hardship.

The fourth argument is the importance of marriage in society. The government sees marriage as important. It gives specific rights and benefits to married couples. Denying marriage and its privileges to same-sex couples shows that these couples are not equal.

STRAIGHT TO THE
SOURCE

After the decision was announced, Obergefell gave a speech outside the Supreme Court:

> *Today's ruling from the Supreme Court affirms what millions across this country already know to be true in our hearts: our love is equal. That the four words etched onto the front of the Supreme Court—"equal justice under law"—applied to us too. All Americans deserve equal dignity, respect, and treatment when it comes to the recognition of our relationships. . . . It's my hope that the term gay marriage will soon be a thing of the past, that from this day forward it will simply be marriage, and our nation will be better off because of it. I also hope that this decision has a profound effect in reducing the stigma, the hurt, the alienation, and discrimination that LGBT people all too often feel when we live our lives openly.*

Source: J. Bryan Lowder. "Jim Obergefell's Poignant Statement on the Marriage Equality Decision." *Outward.* Slate Group, LLC, n.d. Web. December 18, 2017.

Consider Your Audience

Adapt this passage for a different audience, such as your principal or friends. Write a blog post conveying this same information for the new audience. How does your post differ from the original text and why?

THE DISSENTING OPINION

our justices disagreed with the court. They were John Roberts, Samuel Alito, Antonin Scalia, and Clarence Thomas. Each wrote his own opinion on the decision.

Justice Roberts wrote the principal disagreement. He outlined three arguments against the court's ruling. His first argument was that the court should not make policy decisions. He believed the court should only deal with issues related to the Constitution. Roberts didn't feel that same-sex marriage was one of these issues.

John Roberts is the Supreme Court Chief Justice, the person who leads the business of the court.

Roberts's second argument explains who he thinks should address such matters. He writes that a decision like this should be made by the people. He notes that Supreme Court justices are not elected. Members of the federal and state Congresses are. Roberts says these lawmakers should make decisions on same-sex marriage.

His final argument is that this could lead to more changes in marriage. Roberts suggests that people might next legalize polygamy. Polygamy is the marriage of more than two people. This is illegal in the United States. Roberts thinks same-sex marriage is a

Gay couples also had a long road to gain rights to same-sex adoption. Mississippi was the last state to reverse the ban in 2016.

bigger change from traditional marriage than polygamy would be.

Scalia, Thomas, and Alito

Scalia joined Roberts. He agreed with the points Roberts raised. He wrote that it was inappropriate for the court to make a ruling on same-sex marriage.

Conservative blogger Ed Morrissey wrote a post discussing Scalia's view on the case. He agrees that same-sex marriage is not a matter for the Supreme Court to decide:

What Scalia decries is the court's move to make itself the arbiter of every social and legal issue, whether or not it falls under the federal government's purview, by abusing the Equal Protection Clause of the 14th Amendment, among other devices. It's legislative power without any check or balance, and goes far beyond the boundaries of what the Constitution imagined as a role for the court.

Scalia described the court's actions as a "threat to American democracy."

Thomas talked about the meaning of liberty. He defined liberty as "freedom from government action." This means the government cannot wrongfully imprison or harm someone. He wrote that liberty does not mean people should get benefits from the government.

Gay rights activists continue to fight across the world for equal rights.

TELL ME
AGAIN
HOW WHO
I MARRY
AFFECTS YOU?

Today, the LGBT community continues to fight for equal rights, including for transgender people.

Thomas described the right to same-sex marriage as one of these benefits.

Alito agreed with his fellow judges. He also criticized the majority. He said they forced their beliefs on the nation. He saw this as an attack on people who disagree with same-sex marriage.

Looking Forward

The *Obergefell* decision was a major moment in the history of gay rights. Activists had worked for decades for marriage equality. By the 2010s, public attitudes toward same-sex marriage became more positive than ever. When the Supreme Court took on the case, people on both sides watched closely for the decision.

Same-sex marriage became legal across the country in 2015. But challenges still lay ahead for gay rights activists. New cases and laws threaten gay rights elsewhere. Activists continue working for equality in all areas of life.

IMPORTANT DATES

1924

The Society for Human Rights, first gay rights organization, is formed.

1965

The *Griswold v. Connecticut* decision gives married couples the right to privacy.

1967

The court rules in *Loving v. Virginia* that bans on interracial marriage are illegal.

1969

The Stonewall riots occur in Greenwich Village on June 28.

1986

The Supreme Court rules that relationships between two men are not protected by the Constitution.

1990

Three same-sex couples apply for marriage licenses in Hawaii.

1996

The Defense of Marriage Act (DOMA) is passed by Congress.

2004

Ohio bans same-sex marriage in February.

2013

United States v. Windsor overturns part of DOMA on June 26. On July 22, a federal judge in Ohio rules in favor of Obergefell.

2015

On January 16, the Supreme Court agrees to hear *Obergefell v. Hodges*. On April 28, the Supreme Court hears the *Obergefell* oral arguments. On June 26, the Supreme Court rules in favor Obergefell and same-sex marriage is legalized in the United States.

STOP AND THINK

Tell the Tale

Chapter One discusses an event known as the Running of the Interns. Imagine you are a young news network employee involved in this tradition. Write 200 words about your experience.

Surprise Me

This book discusses the Supreme Court. What two or three facts about the Supreme Court did you find most surprising? Write a few sentences about each fact. Why did you find each fact surprising?

Dig Deeper

After reading this book, what questions do you still have about same-sex marriage? With an adult's help, find a few reliable sources that can help you answer your questions. Write a paragraph about what you learned.

GLOSSARY

activism
actions to support an issue or cause

appeal
to bring to a higher court for review

argument
a reason to support a point of view

custody
a relationship that allows parents or guardians to make decisions for a child

discrimination
poor treatment of a person based on who they are

dissent
disagreement with a decision

inherit
to receive something after the death of a family member

intern
a student working in a job to gain experience

LGBT
lesbian, gay, bisexual, and transgender

opinion
a decision reached by a court

polygamy
marriage between more than two people

ruling
an official decision

ONLINE
RESOURCES

To learn more about the legalization of same-sex marriage, visit our free resource websites below.

Visit **abdocorelibrary.com** for free Common Core resources for teachers and students, including vetted activities, multimedia, and booklinks, for deeper subject comprehension.

Visit **abdobooklinks.com** for free additional online weblinks for further learning. These links are routinely monitored and updated to provide the most current information available.

LEARN
MORE

Bausum, Ann. *Stonewall: Breaking Out in the Fight for Gay Rights*. New York: Viking, 2015.

Petersen, Christine. *How the Judicial Branch Works*. Minneapolis, MN: Abdo, 2015.

ABOUT THE AUTHORS

Duchess Harris, JD, PhD

Professor Harris is the chair of the American Studies department at Macalester College and curator of the Duchess Harris Collection of ABDO books. She is the author and coauthor of recently released ABDO books including *Hidden Human Computers: The Black Women of NASA*, *Black Lives Matter*, and *Race and Policing*.

Before working with ABDO, she authored several other books on the topics of race, culture, and American history. She served as an associate editor for *Litigation News*, the American Bar Association Section of Litigation's quarterly flagship publication, and was the first editor in chief of *Law Raza*, an interactive online journal covering race and the law, published at William Mitchell College of Law. She has earned a PhD in American Studies from the University of Minnesota and a JD from William Mitchell College of Law.

Christina Eschbach

Christina Eschbach graduated from the University of Minnesota, Twin Cities. She lives in Minnesota and works as a software engineer.

INDEX